C000144430

GREATEST
HITS

The New Issues Press Poetry Series

Editor	Herbert Scott
Associate Editor	David Dodd Lee
Advisory Editors	Nancy Eimers, Mark Halliday William Olsen, J. Allyn Rosser
Assistant to the Editor	Rebecca Beech
Assistant Editors	Scott Bade, Allegra Blake, Becky Cooper, Jeff Greer, Gabrielle Halko, Matthew Hollrah, Nancy Hall James, Alexander Long, Tony Spicer, Bonnie Wozniak
Editorial Assistants	Kevin Oberlin, Matthew Plavnick Diana Valdez
Business Manager	Michele McLaughlin
Fiscal Officer	Marilyn Rowe

The New Issues Press Poetry Series is sponsored by The College of Arts and Sciences, Western Michigan University, Kalamazoo, Michigan

An Inland Seas Poetry Book

 Inland Seas poetry books are supported by a grant from The Michigan Council for Arts and Cultural Affairs.

First Edition, 1998.

ISBN: 0-932826-63-6

Library of Congress Cataloging-in-Publication Data:
Sheehan, Marc
Greatest Hits / Marc Sheehan
Library of Congress Catalog Card Number (98-066490)

Art Direction	Tricia Hennessy
Design:	Tricia Hennessy and Gordon Martin, Jr.
Cover Drawing:	Don Adleta
Production:	Paul Sizer The Design Center, Department of Art College of Fine Arts Western Michigan University
Printing:	Bookcrafters, Chelsea, Michigan

GREATEST HITS

MARC SHEEHAN

New Issues Press

WESTERN MICHIGAN UNIVERSITY

Contents

Acknowledgments

Thanks to the editors of the following journals in whose pages these poems first appeared, often in earlier versions:

Apalachee Quarterly: "On Reading Nietzsche in the Factory Canteen."

American Literary Review: "More Than We Can Say For Ourselves."

Chester H. Jones Awards, 1995: "Concerning Lansing, The Capital Of Michigan, And How I Came To Live Here."

Cincinnati Poetry Review: "My Father's Singing."

cold-drill: "St. Patrick's Church."

Damaged Wine: "The 1933 Chicago World's Fair."

Gulfstream: "Pisces."

High Plains Literary Review: "With Three Young Women In The Darkness."

McGuffin: "Grass Fires," "Night Crawlers," "On Being An Adult," "Thanksgiving."

Parting Gifts: "The Empty Present," "The New World Order," "Shame."

Pennsylvania Review: "Pheasant Season."

Pre-Press Awards Vol. 2: "Liner Notes."

Sky: "The Off Season," "Second Marriage."

Sundog: "Later That Same Day."

Sycamore Review: "The Living."

"The Cursive World" was originally a chapbook published by Ridgeway Press.

Many of these poems were written with the help of grants from the Michigan Council for the Arts (now the Michigan Council for Arts and Cultural Affairs), and the National Endowment for the Arts.

The author wishes to thank the Cranbrook Writers Guild, the Dyer-Ives Foundation, the Avery Hopwood and Jule Hopwood Foundation, as well as teachers and friends too numerous to mention individually.

Liner Notes

Introducing "Father" John McCray

nicknamed for the blessed way
he could croak out old folk songs,
chanteys, blues or ballads,
for his hummingbird-fast flat picking,
the way he could claw-hammer a banjo,
blow the soul out of a mouth harp
or lift a broken fiddle to his chin
and make the music come out whole.
He played on street corners for change
when the mints still coined real silver
graced with the faces of Greek gods.
No one noticed when he went electric,
rocking the honky-tonks with raucous gospel
made secular for the sins of Saturday.
You may have heard the story of how
he disappeared after the last set
he played to entertain a throng of rowdy
tobacco-chewing children at a beer tent.
With a last twang and groaned-out note
he staggered offstage and didn't come back
to acknowledge the almost rhythmic
foot-stamps and claps of the drunken crowd.
The only body he left behind
are these few rare recordings, recorded live,
the last to be pressed into wax before
this company gets digital equipment.
You can hear the cheers,
the boos, the yelled requests,
cell doors slamming shut, and in one
especially haunting song the sound
of wind moaning over an open mike
and into a stand of jack pines.

On His Fondness for the Fiddle

True story. The concert violinist
Branislaw Huberman had his Stradivarius
stolen by a man who played it
in dark bars and criminal cafes.
Years later, the Strad with yellowed
newspaper clippings of the crime lining
the violin case came to light
only after the fiddler thief had died.
Father claimed to have met the man
in a dank Paris nightclub during
a tour he made as a headliner's sideman.
He said he knew even then that something
other than talent was gracing the way
the man played his bad standards.
After the man's death the Strad
had to be cleaned and an ugly
crack repaired to restore the master's craft.
This is an image, McCray used to say,
of the soul's sojourn in the world.
Creation, grace, exile and return.
We can only know the first
three of these, which is why
God decreed there should be blues—
a form which the violin finds
it can sometimes be content with if
the world calls strongly enough.

Stage Fright

In one of the dreams which haunted him
the rickety stage he's playing on
falls away board by board until
he's perched on a single plank balanced
between two rain barrels racing
downstream toward the falls.
In the other, he has his tiny hands
wrapped around a ukulele playing
for his father from a kitchen table stage.
During the vamp of "Frankie and Johnnie" he looks
down to see that his father has cut
off his baby toes and is rolling
them around with some peas.
Hence his preference for substantial
platforms away from the rabble:
folk festivals, state fairs, jamborees—
outdoor events where there was plenty of air
to pump in and out of his lungs.
Worst were sportsmen's bars and storefront clubs
with postage stamp-sized stages which threatened
to send him shaking into the wings, which in
most of these places meant the alley out back.
Strangely, he was always steely-nerved
before a show, never needing a drink or refusing
to go on for anything other than lack
of the cash he was promised up front.
He always saved his breakdowns for later.
Sometimes, no amount of applause could coax an encore
once his feet found solid ground again.

9

Journal Entry

These small Midwestern towns make me want to settle down—
buy some shack within walking distance of the local tavern, yet
out beyond the halo of the last streetlight. I think about what
Ry Cooder said in talking about a song writer he admired. "In his
songs," Ry said, "you can hear mariachi from the cantina, but also
something deeper, out beyond the city limits. Something like
wind whistling down the arroyos." These villages don't harbor the
bravado and ennui of border towns, but the wind's still another
language, musical and furtive, and I'd have to change my life
entirely to learn it.

Lyrics to "Separation"

Divorce the body from the mind,
Leave the thinking part behind.
Oh baby, baby, yes it's true,
This is what I'm tryin' to do.

Here's the body, there's the soul,
Here's the thread and there's the hole.
Here's the sleeve and there's the arm,
Here's the cold and there's the warm.

Here's the wheat, there's the chaff,
Here's the mouth, there's the laugh.
Here's the word, there's the deed,
Here's the vein, there's the bleed.

Here's the tree, there's the leaves,
Here's the warp, there's the weave.
Here's the salesman, there's the wheedle,
Here's the spoon and here's the needle.

You're the headline, all the news,
I'm the back page obit blues.
You're the princess, I'm the toad.
You're the river and I'm the road.

Take the lock and take the key,
Take the salt and take the sea.
Leave the question, leave the rust,
Leave the Bible and leave the dust.

Divorce the body from the mind,
Leave the thinking part behind.
Oh baby, baby, yes it's true,
This is what I'm tryin' to do.

The Dream

The fruit on the Tree of Life were musical instruments: delicate violins, mature violas, juicy cellos and the almost overripe, limb-bending double basses. It was harvest season and some of the windfallen fruit was already returning to dirt, giving off the sweet smell of decaying music which attracted the lovely humming of bees. With a simple twist—the way an apple, for instance, is picked—the music of the earth fell into the musician's hand, and for a moment he actually cradled one natural guitar in his arms. Ever since, in the waking world, when asked how tunes came to him, he liked saying the best ones seemed as though they were always already in the air. All he had to do was find the right place to stand—somewhere downwind of the sweet notes—until he could hum what he heard.

Curtain Call

On the street he finds a roll
of money and stolen betting slips,
but not even the dreadlocked Rasta
who hands him a blank tract
can keep him from blowing his windfall
on dismal gin in a dim lounge
where he can't seem to read the writing
chalked on a night-black
slate behind the bar.
Where is the red-haired woman who was with him
at the last dance club as the band was setting
up in a dusty ballroom?
Why did he pinch a mandolin
from among the musicians' instruments?—
It has to be bowed instead of plucked
and is tuned to an unearthly scale.
That's his axe the last time I see him
playing for change near a heating grate,
improvising for himself an afterlife,
while the battered case
open at his feet
fills with luminous coins until
even the steam and his sweat shine.

Yang

My Father's Singing

When I right the overturned ash can,
or lift the broken ribbed boat,
then the crickets which are
the night's voice scatter.
Alone they make their lonely scrapings,
their tiny lullabies.

So how can I listen for a single
voice among so many, a voice
unable to lift a ragged hymn alive;
yet in dreams or the green,
unearthly light of the dashboard
he sang unembarrassed to his child?

The crickets' chirping rose to a whine
when we sped through a summer night
while cicadas in their insistence climbed
out of themselves so that we
were for a moment no longer
able to hear them.

Surely this was better
than sleeping undisturbed,
rocked upon the night's waters,
since those carefully caged songs,
those hoardings of good luck,
were loosed and given voice.

The water-logged boat will not
catch fire on the shore.
The crows which plagued the summer
have stayed to see the fall.
And in the dry grass under the elm,
husks that had been song.

Fort Knox, Kentucky, 1966

Clad in green fatigues, red-faced with
103 degree fever, foam ear plugs from
the firing range still in place,

my brother half-staggers to the Falcon,
tells me he doesn't know where the gold is,
says another degree and he'll be in sick bay.

Twelve years old and so naive I don't know
why my brother and his wife want
to be left alone in the motel room.

Back in the Falcon my father turns and turns
trying to find an all-night diner.
Was there, somewhere, a train's fading whistle?

Were soldiers at that very moment changing
guard duty at the doors of great vaults?
Might their marriage have survived

had my brother's wife conceived that night?
Unanswerable questions I plan to ask
a good novelist—or God, if given the chance.

Eighteen months later, home in Michigan,
shivering though spring is unseasonably warm,
he shows us the silk-backed dragon jacket

and a pocketful of strange-charactered coins
which might buy a night in Saigon,
or a gold Buddha made of brass.

Angora

for Jeff Garrity

Jeff snaps the electric scissors to life
and starts underneath, around a goat's penis,
then down its legs, revealing front knees
calloused from unreligious kneeling.
Then comes hog-tying to shear sides and back
and at last he trims the fine angelic hair
grown long over almost human eyes.
Afterwards, the rams rear back and butt heads
to see who in their new skin is king.
You will say men are just like that.
Still, in good times you can get someone to buy
even hair from the belly stained with urine
which would turn golden if it were rinsed out.
Maybe by next spring things will improve—
more kids, less blood, a blade that doesn't dull,
someone to alchemize this pile of foul wool
now filling one large size brown paper bag.

Wild Mushrooms

My ex-wife's Czech grandfather could spot
all the edible ones—

the basement of his Chicago barbershop was strung
with loops of them threaded together.

Expensive, weighed out by the ounce.
Restaurants pricey enough to require them

were out of our range for anything except
major anniversaries.

With a sackful culled from
pine groves north of Muskegon

we spiced up our usual Ragu,
added earthiness to omelettes which

makes tame mushrooms pale.
Half the reason he went back home,

I think, was to pick
the old country's *houby*.

He should have taught someone before it was too late.
I, for one, am sure I couldn't tell

a morel from an Angel of Death—
or at least not distinctions any finer.

We could have sold them to gourmands,
turned bourgeois in our tastes,

though the last plastic bag of them
burned in our freezer.

Thanksgiving

The question as always is just how close
to the headwaters we have to trace a thing,
as when the wounded deer staggered in to
a shallow bend of the Coldwater River
just as we were getting ready to meet
my sister's new partner who ended up
wading in past two failed marriages,
her flirtations with petty theft, a car crash,
unpaid family loans, late-night parties,
unlettered disappearances, and now
a Thanksgiving dinner being kept warm
and a Lions game flickering away
in an empty living room, so he could put
the deer out of its suffering with one
well-aimed blow of a short-handled, twelve pound
sledge hammer to its antlerless head,
as well as to convince us by the way
he did this smoothly without spooking the doe
or having to repeatedly hammer
the animal until it crumpled so we
could drag it out of the freezing water
that beneath his shy thick-handedness here
at last was a man who could handle a heart's
unforeseen turns and plunges over stones.

Second Marriage

They wake up in the room above the chapel
which this time around is their living room—
the flower girl and ring bearer still
asleep in their adjoining pastel sanctums
dreaming of their various parents.
Somewhere the best man is dressed in red,
crouched beneath a stark maple this first day
of deer season—grey morning of low clouds.
At home the maid of honor pads cold
linoleum and laces coffee with scotch.
Last night the bride wondered into sleep
over whether to wear her first wedding gown,
or the blue of her best friend's betrothal.
The groom knows that by the time the honeymoon
has waned the Catholics will already
have resurrected their chipped nativity,
which makes him think back to the claws he removed
from his neighbor's old bathtub to halo
the Madonna she planted in her back yard.
They know now there are partings before death.
They suspect that winning tickets and health
would be better than *for poorer* and croup.
Still, they have new rings and a baby sitter
so they can spend a week-end in Pentwater.
They have fifths of whiskey, liters of soda
and a refrigerator which is lit
from within by huge bowls of coleslaw.
They will have the instant memory of photographs
that develop by themselves, and cake
layered with icing and topped by plastic bells.
The minister will ask if anyone objects and tell
the groom that he needn't slip him that fifty.
But they couldn't get a plumber for that much

and besides the groom knows how to fix almost
anything he can work a wrench around.
And what he doesn't know he is determined
this time to figure out, or live with broke.

On Reading Nietzsche in the Factory Canteen

Almost twenty years later my mind's eye still sees
the smudged paperback cover of the *Portable Nietzsche*.
It was part of the lunch box feast I had after
mornings of working with shafts packed in dry ice,
or learning the intricate gear-guts of the hob spliner,
or lowering rotors into the slurry's black abrasive,
or using the pneumatic lift to hook and swing
another huge bronze government contract casting onto
the industrial washer's chain-link conveyor belt.
No matter how hard I scrubbed with washroom brushes
the page edges gained a layer of black gilt,
so I gave up rubbing my hands raw for naught.

For all Friedrich taught me I should have spent
my lunch hours with Jesus drinking tequila from
a wide-mouthed Mason jar in the parking lot,
or dived into the dirt of porno mags machinists had
stashed in the lowest drawer of their huge tool cribs.
But I slogged through with the *Ubermensch* fueled by
shot-sized paper cups of vending machine tea.
Whatever Zarathustra spoke isn't even echo now,
though if I still had that book I bet I could
still smell the factory on it like a waft of bad air.
But it was a part of my portable library I left behind
to lighten the load for one of my dozen hungry moves.

The Wine Spectator

Because my sun sign, my moon sign,
and half my planets are in Scorpio,
because I paid a full day's

wages to a woman to find this out,
and because I'm at Partners in Wine
buying for a writer's signing

party at the bookstore I work for,
I'm especially attentive when
a biker with *Scorpions* emblazoned

on the back of his black leather jacket
(as well as a patch
with *Detroit* embroidered on it)

asks about California chardonnays.
He has chrome chains and iron
crosses adorning his jacket's flaps;

he has Harley Davidson's
mean eagle sewn over
his left breast pocket.

He thinks the vintner might be Rodney
Strong, but he's not sure.
He strokes his black goatee and seems

too polite to point out to the tight-lipped
sales clerk how little help he's being.
After the biker says good-bye,

I decide finally on white and buy a case
of a Chilean blend after
the clerk says the wine is nicely

balanced.

On Being an Adult

I'm sitting at my terminal in the office
of the American Red Cross in Lansing,
Michigan, thinking about Arthur Rimbaud
who at half my age gave up writing to run
guns to . . . North Africa, I think it was.
(A photo of him posing with his brother, both
of them stiff in their communion suits, graced
the liner notes of Patti Smith's *Easter* album.)
I seem to remember a silence so complete
he didn't even write letters from whatever
corner of the earth it was that he hid in.

I saw in last Sunday's *News* that the hundredth
anniversary of the poet's death
is being celebrated by runners passing
his poems instead of a baton as they race
from his home town through the countryside to Paris.
But since in America we don't read poems
I'm going back to printing letters to donors
thanking them for giving us so much of their blood,
instead of thinking about Arthur Rimbaud—
the damned French poet whose poems I don't
even pretend to understand anymore—
who was wounded by his friend, the poet Paul Verlaine,
and who died at the age I am this year.

Concerning Lansing, the Capital of Michigan, and How I Came to Live Here

The circuits of that 1960 Christmas
gift were primitive, but what I'd wished for—
by putting a cardboard template over
a shiny silver tray I was able
to match up the different kinds of buildings
which people built: the igloos of Eskimos,
Egyptian pyramids, Indian tepees.
I imagined life with the Eiffel Tower
as skyline, or the Empire State Building
or the curled onion domes of Moscow.
By touching the little silver nipples
which fit through holes in the cardboard with a pair
of blunt plastic-handled needles I could
light up a red light when I rightly wedded
Pierre to the state of South Dakota,
or placed Poseidon—draped in kelp and wielding
his mighty trident—on his sea god throne.
After a while I knew the circuits by heart,
and it became like riding the bus to school
on the same awful route each day to third grade.
It was the single gift I had which hinted
at the workings of fate, of futures that weren't
the happy trails of cowboys and milkmen,
the singing policeman I wanted to be.
Before the novelty wore off, the card
I came back to again and again was
one on which the bright Greek gods cavorted.
There was mighty Hercules, flawed Achilles,
Zeus in clouds, stag-hunting Diana
and, of course, Cassandra who knew the future
though everyone hardened their hearts against her.

Peep Shows

The Next Unpaved Turn

Instead of buying the *Times*, bagels and lox, and turning on the TV preachers, we go looking for hysterical markers.

We've posed by most of the bronze plaques around: here stood the county's first doctor's house; here the state's first Union force was mustered; here the river turned red with the blood of Chippewas. We've got our tripod and camera with timer, and keep a collection of happy mug shots.

But this morning Amy's out of sorts. I'm covering the back roads, gravel pinging in the wheel wells. I point out a farm's busted pump, but she doesn't want to play the Windmill Game. The mill's fan is broken—only a five-pointer, anyway.

I snap on the radio and tune in Reverend Elmond preaching his gospel of wealth. I'm just starting to pound the wheel to his cadence when Amy reaches over and flips him off.

We drive in silence for a few more miles, sometimes hitting asphalt, but always turning off. Then we come to a little park that's not on the map. It boasts three picnic tables, a trash can, water running out of a culvert, and bingo!—on this site a treaty was signed in 1790.

I'm just about to pop the VW's trunk when I see that Amy's crying her silent, shoulder-heaving cry.

What can I do? I walk to the cement tube spewing water and bounce some pebbles off it. Her sadness isn't historic and laughable, and I'm not sure of the best way back.

Later that Same Day

She sat on a barstool at her kitchen counter, hammer in hand, breaking dinner plates. Before finishing off the cups and saucers she crossed to the refrigerator and grabbed an almost empty bottle of Chablis, shards of china crunching under her feet. It was cheap wine and she liked feeling the bottle's threads for its twist-off cap on her lips.

At a resale shop she bought two blue willowware plates, a glass candle holder and a souvenir Grand Canyon coffee mug.

That night she made chicken scampi while listening to folk music on the public radio station. She remembered a bottle of champagne a friend had given her, and she popped the cork while some guitar player raced through "Under the Double Eagle."

She diced a chicken breast and a small tomato, juiced half a lemon, chopped some parsley, sliced a couple scallions, and minced a clove of garlic until it was fine as kosher salt. The second clove she crushed by laying the broad knife flat on top of it and bringing her fist sharply down.

Half a bottle of champagne made it harder for her to keep her balance on the broken china.

Folk music changed to jazz, and jazz to classical; she ate the scampi over yesterday's cold fettuccini.

A freak spring ice storm and power outages headlined the late news, followed by the homeless and the dead. As she raised the gaudy coffee mug with the last of the champagne to her lips in the TV's blue light she noticed how her fingers still smelled of garlic. Almost as pungent as sex, she thought, almost as good.

The New World Order

She is soaking in the bathtub when she hears him on the radio—the man who plays music using only his hands.

Back when she and a college boyfriend used to cruise for garage sales they'd bought a world globe from this same man who was giving up his law practice to perform in Vegas.

That evening she'd lit a joint and spun the world while her boyfriend figured out how to make farting sounds by squeezing the air out from between his joined hands. Then they'd sung "He's Got the Whole World in His Hands," which quickly broke down into laughter and groping.

How out of date it must be! Before the radio variety show the news was of hatred fueling war in the former Yugoslavia.

When they split up they'd taken turns choosing the things they'd bought together. He took the broken toaster and the stained old globe while she chose the bike and their stereo. He'd kept saying, "No, I really want this. Really."

She would like to again finger the Himalayas worn down to cardboard, the long coffee stain floating out in the Atlantic.

The memory of that globe and toaster stuffed into an orange crate with the worst of their records finally makes it possible for her to cry. She has wanted to for weeks, thinking of how out of love she has fallen.

She is weeping in great, satisfying gulps when her husband knocks on the door and asks what's going on in there.

She splashes water on her face and when she is able she reports on the slaughter of innocents.

First Marriage

They found their rings in a velvet-lined box of costume jewelry in a head shop just off campus. Their wedding photos show the two of them wearing the tell-tale goofy grins of very good Columbian.

Within days the rings turned the skin on their fingers an unhealthy looking gray, so they embarked upon what they called their Ringless Marriage.

There was a huge futon covered with an Indian print cloth, and an American flag tacked to the ceiling to shade a bare bulb. There was smoke—from joints, from burned curry, from a hibachi on a rickety rain-worn table on the tiny patio of their third floor efficiency—a pungent haze which made them feel their mid-west college town might almost be Calcutta, or Tangier.

They went to a free summer screening of *Casablanca* and left in the middle to make love.

In cut-offs and sunglasses they played inelegant tennis on the deserted courts behind the stadium until other students began returning for the fall term.

They told themselves that it didn't matter, that nothing, really, had changed—not even when one or the other would come home late. They decided upon 'at the library' as an acceptable lie.

By mid-semester the leaves were off the trees and morning frost outlined them on the campus sidewalks. He was learning how Shakespeare's weather established mood, how an October sky became a blue you couldn't avoid.

Rodin on Loneliness

The university art museum is quiet. A few students drift in and then back out again, but only one young man smelling of marijuana studies anything with more than passing interest.

Except for the woman.

She is sitting on a low marble bench staring at a figure by Rodin. At her side is a shiny black vinyl purse she should have checked at the desk, but the undergraduate working there let the motherly looking woman walk right past.

The bronze figure is lying on its side with one partial arm outstretched, which makes it appear that it might be trying to swim—or fly? A small sign informs the woman that this was a rejected part of Rodin's ambitious and unfinished *Gates of Hell*.

Notice the hack-saw scars on the figure's back, the sign says.

The gallery's single guard wonders what she's doing here—they don't draw in many non-students.

She could have wandered in from viewing a body at the funeral home just off campus—the help here has seen it before—but she isn't teary-eyed or distraught. She seems content to try to imagine the sculpture in its original setting, among smooth-finished sinners.

She hits the sidewalk just as students are pouring out of classrooms. They surge and eddy around her, sometimes arm-in-arm, or else stop to kiss before rushing on.

Shame

Our hero stumbles out of the smoky strip club and into a cold February wind.

When he turns his car key there is only a disheartening click. His headlights burned while he watched the strippers dance. Two in particular: a tall blonde who kept rubbing her hands on her skimpy leotard to get a better grip on the brass pole she sometimes climbed; and another, more petite, who wore a black teddy and had a thickly bandaged left hand.

He could call his ex-wife. She would come and give him nothing worse than a good connection and a wrinkled glare. He would rather go back inside, back to the stripper who, for only a dollar, dropped her halter top in front of him, revealing her blue-veined breasts.

He has read about the extinction of certain emotions. 'Forbearance', for example. What he feels now is something like shame but less definite, with fewer possibilities.

Finally he asks two stocky, smirking college-age kids to give him a jump. They don't have cables, but they push his car and just before it reaches a snow bank he pops the clutch and the engine catches.

As he stamps the gas pedal he feels delivered into a state of uncertain grace.

It's really not so cold, and if he drives a few extra blocks the car will probably start for him should he decide to make another stop.

The Empty Present

On the second day of the new year, Harrington decides to put up his tree. As he stands hungover in his living room drinking a cup of bad black coffee, he sees that most of his neighbors have already put their scotch pines and blue spruces on the curb.

Harrington drains his mug, slides a pair of deck shoes onto his bare feet, cinches his bathrobe and steps outside. It's Saturday morning and people are either sleeping late or else taking leave of relatives—hatchbacks packed with children.

Leaving old Mrs. Edward's tree on his living room floor, he clomps to the basement and finds a dusty tree stand. Mercifully, the tree stands up after he's screwed the two together.

He pours another cup of coffee, laces it with whiskey, and scuffs his way up to the attic.

His ex has most of the decorations, but a bag of wrapping paper holds a few small shiny globes and some paper snowflakes.

It's noon by the time he hangs these and drinks another laced coffee. He changes and walks to a corner store where he buys a box of discounted lights and a carton of egg nog.

On his way home he watches a station wagon pull into its driveway. A back door opens and a young girl bounces out, followed by a black Lab who runs circles around her.

Amazingly, all the lights work. He wonders why there's no rum for the eggnog, or anything to put in the box he begins to wrap.

Human/Nature

The 1933 Chicago World's Fair

The 200 foot tall Havoline
Motor Oil Company
thermometer read 83 degrees.

Incongruous to that
Century of Progress
where even the smooth art deco

buildings were built for speed,
the Ball Canning Company
employed my mother to man

their booth showing various
pears and relishes
preserved in cool blue jars.

Center stage was Sally Rand
the woman who stole the show
(her *nom de plume* taken from

an atlas of road maps)
who danced to "Clair de Lune"
employing only two cleverly used

ostrich feather fans.
In that ephemeral Byzantium
the Hall of Science unveiled

its glittering predictions,
the Avenue of Flags snapped in the wind,
and the Transparent Man, his organs

viewable as last summer's fruit,
raised his veined face and arms
as if imploring the anxiously awaited

future to arrive.

Pisces

My cousin spilled the plastic bucket of bullhead minnows
into the lake whose only stock until then was
bluegill, sunfish, pickerel and bass.
Now when I sit with my mother on the rotting dock
they're all we pull up—hand sized, inedible—
on the end of our flimsy bamboo poles.
Bullheads have sharp, pointed fins,
and when we land one that's taken the bacon-scrap
baited hook too deeply, my mother gets the fish
under her rubber sole and does what
she has to get the hook loose, kicking the eviscerated
fish back half-dead to the lily pads.
A friend of mine who fishes for sport files
the barbs from off his hooks to hone
his skill, and for the flash
a healthy rainbow has on its release.
He's such a big man—massive—that his gentleness is as
surprising as my mother's . . . what? Callousness?
Oh sometimes you just have to live, enjoying
how a clear sky darkens into starlight
instead of trying to find words to contain it:
cornflower, robin's egg, violet, indigo, lazuli, onyx . . .
Just cut the line from this whiskered fish
who's taken the bait and let him live
with a rusting question mark throbbing in his jaw.

Night Crawlers

Nights after afternoon cloudbursts or early
evening showers our headlights rake them,

whole families of bent-backed Asians,
flashlights in hand, shining night crawlers.

Or we spot them beneath infrequent street lights,
coffee tins stuffed full of shredded news,

searching the vacant lots of razed houses
littered with bricks and broken boards.

Their gleaning is elemental and un-American,
though I once knew a woman who lived in a ramshackle

farm house surrounded by a graveyard
who sold night crawlers from out of her parlor.

I don't recall ever buying that bait
in hopes of landing a state record catch,

something miraculously Midwestern,
symbolic of the afterlife, unencumbered love . . .

No, that miracle's in the future,
now, or nowhere.

With Three Young Women in the Darkness

All summer has seen such distance.
Now it's just this broken swing,
one chain unlinked so that its seat
dangles down its useless wing.
I'm just that far from the closest
of three young women scything the air.
There should always be such joy
in our affairs with the earth
as there is in these foot-scrapings,
these hollows our too-long-leggedness
builds beneath each swing.
Could we construct such smooth
and gentle graves as these?
After rising from the cool grass
where we land after our almost
obligatory leap from the apex
of our imaginary scythes' sweep,
we walk over the bridge which still
anchors the ruined sluice gate,
and into and through the gardens.
One girl has small breasts, one is
short while the third is just
the sway of a skirt in waning light.
If not for me would there
be secrets they could share?
Would they pick our gracious
host's hybrid flowers to weave
into each other's hair?
All of my words have been wrong;
I might as well have spat
out mouthfuls of apple-rot.
I should have kept my silence.
When we return it's to lamplight.

I feel I have wounded this
memory for them, unbalanced
the scale of starlight with my need.
But in the morning the short
girl asks as we leave, "Wasn't
that a fun walk last night?"
Perhaps I am not as graceless
as I'd thought. Perhaps I really
don't need to wear these weeds.

Grass Fires

for Tom Lynch

Started either by farmers whose soil bank
fields needed their saplings burned away,
or by young punks (though old as their parents now)
who flipped lit cigarettes used as fuses
to light packs of matches in brown fields
once their hot rods were halfway into town,
they often got beyond the stage where we
could slap them back with blankets and gunny sacks
soaked with hoses or dipped into sinkholes,
and so brought long sirens and township pump trucks.

One dry spring a fire jumped a fence row
and raced its way to the parish graveyard.
Hillens, O'Connors, Connellys and Sheehans:
I heard that these children of immigrants
had never wholly lost the brogues which were
faint heirlooms inherited from parents.
Ah, someone surely caught hell from the priest
for letting the weeds be high enough to burn.
I'm a practical man; I'll be ashes
though I saw the grass could not stay dead for long.

Pheasant Season

In October cock pheasants would flame from roadsides
like frenzied resurrections of fallen leaves.
Those decorative Chinese court birds are stuffed now
in Sportsmen's Bars or printed on faded wallpaper,
even blown into glass and filled with bourbon so that hens
commemorate the sour distillation of a wasted summer.
For that corn is reaped now, a little spared,
so that the dry wings of their ghostly leaves may flap
as though trying to rise above the sorry bamboo
of their bodies. But what rose were pheasants
from fields worthless as their tassels of blown silk.
Even now they evoke the loneliness of Midwestern autumns,
those ring-necks, first released below Portland.
From China to the Northwest to Michigan. The soul

itself never imagined its trip into the body as stranger
than a ferry ride on tramp steamer or teak junk
across sickening moon tide surges of pacific water.
And then at Thanksgiving when we ate the corn-fed pheasant
taken cleanly on the wing, we spat out pellets of birdshot
onto the luminous moons of grandmother's bridal china.
Perhaps it was only the body's tide we swam up from,
though I had a friend who, with only a pocket knife,
would carve pieces of broken cornstalks for
the bodies of what he called his "bird calls." It was
an awful soul he could blow out of them, almost
like a gaudy pheasant's, a peacock's raucous caw,
almost like the cry we used to raise from long blades of grass
stretched taut between the thumbs and held to the mouth
delicately as the cup of a hunter's hands
cradling a match in a chill wind.

The Off Season

The summer homes have been closed and shuttered.
The fish house is a faint smell and a sign
for smoked coho and next spring's charter boats.
The fishwife looks so disconcertingly like
an old lover that for a moment you think
about staying to see Lake Michigan freeze.
The cement fountain is drained and filled
with dry leaves whose color the last tour of
tourists took back with them downstate in snapshots.
In the Family Tavern old men complain
about the weather, lost love and strawberries.
There are shiny new CD's in the jukebox
(no one plays them), and pickled eggs on the bar.
There's a final concert at the opera house—
restored with money from the Arts Council—
but it's local folks playing for relatives.
Some of the summer places are mansions,
though most are clapboard boxes. Either way
if home is where you write the rent check, then
you settle for the local bed and breakfast.
Even with the cut in rates they've thrown in
an extra helping of silence and all
the longing you can stand to bring back for free.

More Than We Can Say for Ourselves

For Ruby Hoy Murawski

Home is where, we decided, one drunken
evening you'll remember, our hearts grew up.
So yesterday, home for an uncle's funeral,
I took a walk around the sinkhole lake
to find what that vulture was circling,
catching whatever thermal drafts there are
at the end of this bitter November.
And yesterday I saw again how the land
around the lake is bowl-shaped, eroded,
how the ice-filmed water was once much higher.
That's when I began thinking of you and how
the only thing that makes stones precious here
is their memory, their fossil imprint
of our prehistory, of fiddlehead
ferns which have preserved their frozen notes.
What did I find among the thornapples?
A crow. Perched on one branch and leaning
on another, he seemed ready for flight.
And though the chill wind last night blew him down
to die, it left him in air, his element.

St. Patrick's Church

Seen from a swale the whitewashed steeple
rises right out of a wheat field.
The most distant row of graves is lost
in a tangle of wild grape vines.
Who could desire a different life?—
Even those old world ones,
say Yeats or Joyce, or else Parnell.
This is where the best man of
a doomed marriage gets laid out
faint among the stones and where
rumors about the good father's love
of real estate take on flesh.
Here the wind lifts the white lace
from off my sister's head and snags it
just out of reach in a thorn tree.
Here John Troy whose death I won't
remember parks his huge Studebaker
in the sun which makes the smell
of fresh laundry stronger than leaking oil—
it must be our month to house him now
that the wind has twisted his home.
The steeple's cross was nailed in place
by my grandfather who had to stand
on another man's shoulders since that man
already stood on the ladder's top rung.
It will hold sway for twenty more years
until the ashes are raked away,
leaving room enough in the graveyard
for planting the last parishioners—
those whose whole lives were spent
in the county of Kent, in Michigan.

The Living

A cloud of birds rises from behind a tractor
as though its plow had released them from
a winter of waiting in the earth.
Never again will the living
believe that summer begins
with the wave of a homemade wand.
All summer long the barn's only thought
is chaff, as all winter long it was drafts
and diminishment, *getting by*.
Cairns of stones lie beneath shade oaks
all alone among cloddy furrows,
and spirals of wire are so old
their barbs snap right off
leaving fingers dusted with the pollen of rust.
The problem of where the body ends and
the world begins will be
decided, as always, entirely wrong,
since sometimes the sky comes all the way down
to the ground before retreating beyond
the irregular and ever-smaller
rungs of a changing maple.
The house's eyes are all unblinking,
its weather vane points north until
one morning a horse's hooves
scar long sloping dunes of snow.
Dappled, full of fallen starlight,
great clouds of breath rising from his nostrils,
the stallion stamps that frozen field
out behind the sphere of voices.

The Cursive World

Fish

Even in filthy streams   even in rivers
foul as history   downstream from the factories
the sewer mains   that pile of rusting steel drums
even in those holes   where no one sane swims
even here there still linger   stories of fish
(although not trout no   probably not)
old & wise & wily   which the young boys with
their cane poles   or K Mart Zebco combos can't catch
They stay there for years   insistent as imagination
so that a father   home from a shift at the stamping plant
can ask his son if he caught   the Old Man in the river today
& the son says no   I saw 'im though
though the two might not say   another word all night

Snake

slender blue curves crossing   heat-wavered dead end roads
whips young boys crack   strips of green neon
sudden rustlings   quick disappearances into

holes hidden close to   rain-worn gravestones
fingerlings rescued   from puzzled cats
(lifted there they slide   lightly on hedges of mint)

they know the feel of eelgrass   how summer sun tumbles down
deeply into quarries   the way clay cools
and long before poets they knew   the sexuality of stones

Frog

Praised by Issa   transfixed by light
speared by long-handled   three-tipped gigs

I've lugged burlap   sacks full of frog
seen mating frogs raised   together on rusted prongs

listened to the low   groan of their croaking
in stagnant ponds seen   tadpoles grow

out of their sperm-shaped   selves into bulls
every bit as broad as   bison painted in caves

even by the light of   one's third eye
their delicate legs look   almost atrophied

while those bodies we waste   contain the great
throats which make night   resonant with bellows

Whippoorwill

of sparrow more   at home than native birds
of crow cleaning   our road kill
of red wing perching   on roadside cattails
of killdeer shamming   hurt to lure you from its nest

of grosbeak with its   freshwater toucan bill
of hawk whose preying once   shattered my reading of Proust
of jay who in the face of danger   raises its awful song
of cardinal who this morning was   a red rag doll in the cat's
    mouth

of owl's swivel head and   melancholy call
of barn swallow who nested above   our door and dove at us
of dove linked indissolubly in   my memory with morning
    glories
of martin for whom we build   such extravagant homes

of wren whose house is sometimes just   a box with a quarter-
    sized hole
of woodpecker whose red head drills   for ants that carpenter
    trees
of vulture who even migrates in   its trademark gyre
of veery whose song I've   heard as swirling water

it's only whippoorwill whom I've seen   only in museums
who kept us awake all   night in the spring of its mating
whose three note call became the most   insistent I ever heard
whose usually plaintive scale was that   night filled with the
    need to be

Wasp

daubs mud under eaves   under the peaked tin roof of
St. Patrick's storage shed   (the stored communion hosts are
    soiled)
under cornices against which painters   lean their tall ladders

the gray paper lanterns they live in   hung from tree limbs
don't shine like gaudy   lights outlining patios
nor do they dissolve in rain like painted   parasols made of
    onionskin

swept from the old folks'   attic after the funeral
piled together with dead flies in   little mounds the broom
    builds
the rotten lintels and the sills   of windows which they nested
    are condemned

ungainly as bombers   sluggish in the spring
by August they're frantic   manic as Handel
their gradual unwinding is the most unnoticed   element of
    autumn

Herons

Strange how the heart sinks seeing
                    their plum-colored wings lift
to trace in air the river's bends while small
                    as minnows their reflections skim the Pigeon
then settle on thin stilts
                    to spear fish from muddy shallows
their young wobbly as we'd expect colts
                    sired by Pegasus to be
dark dusky blue which comes from having
                    just fallen from an early evening sky

Walking around a swamp I saw
                    one trapped by wire in a backwash
in the rusted remains of a fence still nailed
                    to a green post in the flooded swale's slime
and by the time I arrived as savior wrapped
                    in leather gloves and waders it
had flown away as the old hymn says
                    the kind of flight
imagination prays for—freeing
                    and graceful against all odds

Turtle

snappers trapped in languid ponds   quick thin rubberbacks
   who flip
themselves upright with pebbly necks   or water-winged in the
   oceans
air-tanked humans holding   on to that watery grace

such patience is unattainable   to flaunt the flow of time
by never changing at all   to be one with the fossil
remnants to be   nearly stone yourself

to hold your breath all winter   to harbor so many
delicate kinds of meat   to outlive Darwin on Galapagos
or exist in wretched pet stores still   gaudy with the paint of
   creation

Dragonfly

The red winged blackbird   does not want
to consider the purely   Jurassic look of the dragonfly

has no need   to compare the dragonfly's wings
to the shape of maple   seeds or dragonflies

themselves to winged walking sticks   it just keeps on
telling me to leave   does not even

bother to drop   the dragonfly he's caught

The Cursive World

Let's say you can recreate on paper
the falcon's sudden plummet,
the dance of grass on the dune which in myth

is a mother bear mourning her twin cubs—
those two islands—who could not reach shore,
the sinuous path of a snake through sand,

an egg-heavy turtle dragging its tail . . .
Let's say these words aren't estranged:
synapse and syntax, water and wave.

Photo credit: Carole Steinberg Berk

Marc J. Sheehan was born in Grand Rapids, Michigan, in 1954. He holds advanced degrees in English from Central Michigan University and the University of Michigan. Such journals as *Michigan Quarterly Review*, *Manhattan Poetry Review*, and *Fine Madness* have published his poetry, essays and reviews. He has been awarded grants from the National Endowment for the Arts and the Michigan Council for the Arts (now the Michigan Council for Arts and Cultural Affairs). He has been a machinist, a bookseller, apartment painter and an instructor at Jackson Community College, Sienna Heights College, and others. At present he works as a Communication and Marketing Specialist for the Great Lakes Region of the American Red Cross Blood Services in Lansing, Michigan, where he also is book reviewer for the *Lansing Capital Times*.